AL[L] MOUNTAIN

Pock'It Instructor

All the skills for all the mountain
Skiing Faster, Bumps, Off-piste, Steeps

Sally Chapman

ALL MOUNTAIN SKIING

The 'All Mountain Pock'It Instructor' identifies which tool is best to use for specific conditions/pistes, encouraging the skiers development and enjoyment of all mountain skiing.

Learn to adapt your technique, control your speed and line at will, switch your focus when required and take on, with confidence, what previously you would have avoided.

Fulfil your skis potential - become a better 'driver'!

Introducing the 2nd book in its series, 'All Mountain Pock'It Instructor' provides tips, techniques and tactics, for the most effective way to tackle all mountain skiing. The book is divided in to four chapters. Each chapter addresses and supplies solutions for the main challenges skiers encounter when skiing the whole mountain.

Pock'It Instructor (book 1) provided a 'tool box' enabling the skier to gain far more pleasure from skiing by improving their ability, confidence and expanding their boundaries. Continuing along similar lines the 'All Mountain Pock'It Instructor' is intended to take that 'tool box' and develop it further.

In the past, ski instruction was restricted, in part, by the ski equipment then available. More recently instruction has evolved to complement modern ski equipment technology. Skis are now designed to aid the 'all mountain' skiing experience. Skis have become shorter, wider and more stable. This means, when skied correctly, the ski will turn/pivot quicker, have greater edge/carve qualities, remain more stable at speed and drive through heavier, off piste conditions more easily. However, without a good 'driver' these skis may just as well be supporting the fence at the back of your garden!

Use this book to improve your skiing, learn how best to tackle specific slopes and conditions, be challenged, be safe and most of all enjoy the all mountain experience.

Sally

ALL MOUNTAIN SKIING

A guide and index to the books contents

Remember, just read or focus on one page, one section or one tip!

SKIING STEEPS

- Pivoting- Use Your Brakes!
- Scrape then Check
- Pole Pressure!
- Jumping/How to Hop
- One Footed Take Off
- QUICK TIPS - for Skiing Steeps

SKIING OFF PISTE MOUNTAIN SAFTEY PAGES

- Stem Step
- Light on Your Feet
- Freeride with Power
- Powder Play
- Deeper, Heavier, Steeper
- QUICK TIPS - for Skiing Off Piste

'TOOL BOX' RE-VISITED

MAKING CURVES

'No straight lines, smooth curves'
Use the design of the ski to control your speed and line.

+

LINKING CURVES

'How you change direction'
Link the curves together by changing the edges and therefore your direction.

+

STEERING CURVES

'Use your steering wheel'
Control your speed and line for the conditions encountered.

+

TERRAIN TACTICS

'Where, when, which?'
Utilise and select the right 'tool' for the right conditions.

=

SKIING

ALL MOUNTAIN SKIING

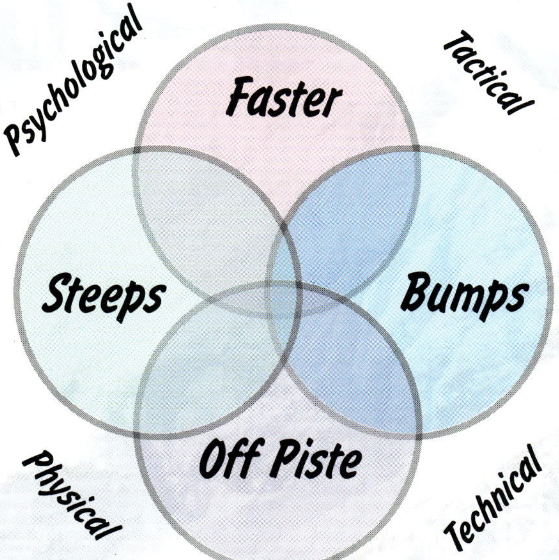

PRE-SKI & APRES SKI

Warming up and lightly stretching before any physical activity is important. Skiing is no different, a little time spent in preparation will help your body, your skiing and potentially prevent needless injury.

N.B If you are injured it is your responsibility to seek professional guidanc and advice in all circumstances.

WARM UP YOUR TEMPERATURE

Use gentle running, walking or jumping.

Squatting

Extending

Gentle Arm Swings

Leg Swings...

...Gently!

Pivoting/Leg Turning

Leg Tilt/Hips

Hip Circles

IMPORTANT TIPS

- Before stretching it is important to raise your body temperature.
- Do not over stretch, gentle stretching and no bouncing.
- When warming up with skis on or off make sure you are in a safe, flat area.
- Don't warm up and then sit on a chair lift for 15 minutes.
- Use time in lift queues, waiting for fellow skiers to warm up.
- Cooling down is as important.

STRETCHES

Hold 10 secs warming up, 25-30 secs cooling down.

Calves

Hamstrings

Legs/Back

SKIING FASTER

This section concentrates on how to focus on and improve carving. Learn to use the ski for what it has been designed, enjoy skiing faster round the curve and not directly down the hill. This provides the sensation of speed, power and control, which will give an awesome ride!

'Carving round Curves' provides the best mental picture for 'skiing faster' with modern skis.

TIPS FOR CARVING

- Select the appropriate slope and gradient.
- Focus on the curve the ski is making on the snow.
- Direct your line using your skill and strength.
- Commit to using your momentum to change edges and direction.

Long Leg/Short Leg

WHY?

- *An Ideal warm up activity to give you the feeling of carving and edging.*
- *Using a small 'wedge' stops you wanting to turn your feet and skis.*
- *Ideal technique to use in soft or slushy snow.*

HOW?

Gain speed down the hill, start to push on the outer ski, allowing the inner leg to bend underneath you.

Push harder against the outer ski through the heel of your foot. The ski bends and deflects you up the hill, whilst accelerating.

Release this pressure and your body will move across your skis.

The skis will change on to the new edges ready for you to push and steer your curve once more.

Outer leg pressure, inner leg stabiliser!
Can you work your pedals?

WHERE?

Open piste, not too steep.

TIPS

Focus

Focus on working the skis and legs independently. Allow the inside leg to bend and soften as you push against the outer ski's edge.

Imagery

The feeling of the legs working independently in carved turns is like the feeling of riding a bicycle up hill. You start to push against the pedal with resistance, the other leg stays relaxed and bends underneath you, ready to take up the next pedal's rotation. You stop pushing on one pedal and prepare to push down against the other pedal.

Feedback

The only difference between using a 'wedge' and being 'parallel' is the turning of the inner ski, the outer ski works exactly the same.

TOP TIP
Think curves, NOT straight lines.

SKIING FASTER

The 'WAITING GAME'

WHY?

- *'Carve', use the design of the ski.*
- *Enjoy speed around the curve, not down the hill.*

HOW?

Push off down the hill to gain momentum. Start to push on the outer ski's edge, creating a curve back up the hill.

Keep strong over your outer foot/ski, keeping the legs apart. Your speed increases around the curve.

When you feel that you need to change direction, stop pushing on the outer ski, release the pressure, soften the leg, DON'T TURN THE FEET/SKIS…… WAIT!

The skis **will** change edges without you turning them, your momentum will do this for you. HONEST!

Start to feel for the outer ski's edge to push against, **don't rush**. Allow the inner leg to bend so you can push harder against the outer ski if necessary.

WAIT! Use your momentum to change your edges and really 'carve'.

WHERE?

Open pisted slope, not too steep and not crowded !

TIPS

Focus

Focus on maintaining the curve shape. When you want to change direction, soften and release the pressure on the ski that you are pushing against. Play the 'WAITING GAME'...until the edges have changed and off you go again...

Imagery

Imagine the outer ski is like the outside wheels of a car speeding around a roundabout. All the pressure is on the outside wheels of the car, with no pressure on the inside wheels.

Feedback

It is tempting to turn the feet/skis once you have stopped pushing on the outer ski. You feel you should be doing something. DON'T. Let your speed and momentum allow the edges to change, have confidence that this will happen. It will, as long as you are making curves and not straight lines.

TOP TIP

Feel the speed around the curve, not down the hill.

Catch the Train

WHY?

- ***A great way to test your skill.***
- ***Learn how to accelerate and decelerate.***
- ***Great fun!***

HOW?

Allow a fellow skier of a similar or slightly better level to lead the way. Make sure you are close behind as soon as the leader sets off.

Concentrate on watching the tracks in the snow of the skier you are following. Follow in these tracks as best you can.

If you are the skier in front try to make your turns rhythmic, concentrate on making curves and gaining speed around the curve not down the hill.

Don't mirror (copy) the skier in front. Concentrate on the line and following.

Following is a great way to gain constant feedback!

WHERE?

Open pisted slope, not busy or too steep.

TIPS

Focus

When following, focus directly on the line of the skier, not the skier themselves. When leading make smooth carved turns, gaining speed around the curve not down the hill.

Imagery

Imagine you are a train with carriages winding down a mountain pass without brakes! Luckily the tracks bend in smooth curves that enable you to control your speed and direction!

Feedback

Finding it difficult to keep up and follow? You are probably turning your skis too much at the start of the turn as you change direction, remember to WAIT, feel for the edge to push against. DON'T TURN THE SKIS/FEET.

TOP TIP
Watch the tracks not the skier!

SKIING FASTER

Outer Foot Power

WHY?

- *Ski faster in variable conditions.*
- *Keep your leg alignment strong and your knees injury free.*

HOW?

Use the design of the ski and pressure control to steer the ski. Do not try to turn the skis/feet to steer, feel for the outer ski's edge to push against.

Allow the inner leg to bend more but maintain contact with the snow for stability.

Stand firm over the outer ski applying pressure down through the heel of your foot. Look where you are going, not down the hill.

As your speed slows release the pressure. Use your momentum or extend the legs, to lighten the skis and change edges.

As soon as the edges have changed stand firm over the outer ski, steering it powerfully through the snow.

Keep strong, steer powerfully, maintain stability.

WHERE?

Wider slopes.
Variable snow conditions.
Slushy snow.

TIPS

Focus

Pressurise through the heel of your outer foot and allow the inner leg to stay relaxed but in contact with the snow.

Imagery

Envisage your body being completely in line with your skis, there are no feelings of being twisted.

Feedback

On changing direction you may feel unbalanced and your speed may slow. To help maintain the speed, pressure and power through the snow, pull your lower arm round to help keep your balance and pressure over the outer ski.

TOP TIP

Drive the skis through the snow, standing strong on the outer ski.

SKIING FASTER

The 'CROSSOVER'

WHY?

- *Use speed and momentum to change direction.*
- *Pure edge to edge skiing.*

HOW?

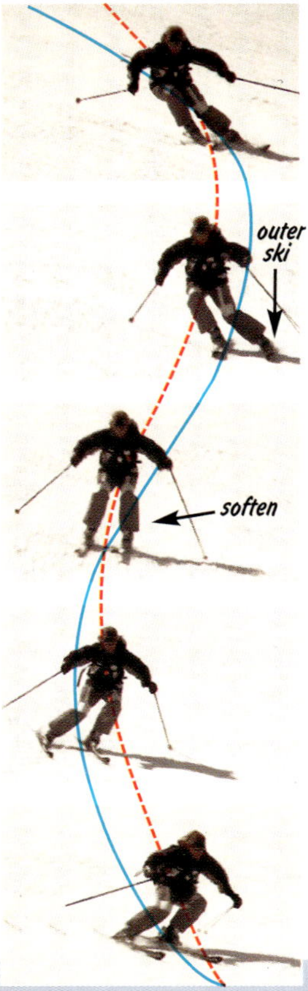

Point the skis down the slope until you have speed.
Keep the feet/legs fairly wide apart and flexed. Tilt the skis on to their edges.

As the skis start to curve and more speed is gained, apply more pressure to the outer ski. Allow the inner leg to bend more.

When you want to change edges and direction stop pushing on the outer ski, soften the outer leg.

As the legs soften, the body will move across the skis, changing the edges.

The skis accelerate on their edges, let them. Maintain strong posture over the skis and be ready to apply pressure and steer the curve once more.

Let the skis take one pathway, whilst your momentum takes the other!

WHERE?

Open, wide pisted slope.

TIPS

Focus

Focus on staying in balance over the skis and not ending up on your edges with no pressure against them.

Imagery

Think of your belly button following one path (red line), whilst the skis follow another (blue line).

Feedback

When speed and momentum increase and the crossover happens quickly, it is easy to fall on to the top ski (banking), losing your balance and the ability to steer the outer ski. Concentrate on maintaining good balance and contact over your outer foot/ski.

TOP TIP

Do not consciously turn the feet/skis, allow the skis to work for you, not against you.

QUICK TIPS!

KEEP CURVING

Always keep steering your curve until you are ready to change direction.

BIG TOE/LITTLE TOE

To help you change direction without pivoting your skis, think of rocking from your big toe of the outer ski to your little toe of the outer ski. This will help release the pressure and change your direction whilst remaining on your edges in order to maintain carving.

LEG LEAN

In order to create more tilt allow your inner leg to bend more underneath you.

PRESSURE RELEASE NOW

When you want to change direction shout **NOW**, allow the legs to soften, release the pressure, **wait**, allow your skis to change edges....then off you go again....

USE THE TERRAIN

Feel through your feet as you travel around the curve, if you hit a small bump or ridge and are ready to change direction use the terrain to change the skis edges and your direction.

SKIING BUMPS

To Ski bumps you need to have the tools available to you that you know will work. These tools will provide you with the control you need, gradually building your confidence and your skill level. Like most skills though, it has to be practised.

This chapter provides you with some techniques, tips and tactics on how best to ski bumps. Whether you want to ski bumps faster or more controlled. Play around with the different tools helping you to master control of your speed and line. You will become more versatile, combining the techniques available to you, so much so, that you will soon be searching for these 'beasts of the piste' rather than hiding from them!

Bumps are formed by skiers skiing short turns, usually, on steeper slopes that are not pisted or, at the side of these pistes. Short turns are used to help control the skiers descent, as more skiers ski the slope with similar rhythms, bumps are formed!

Progression for bump skiing.

- Ski short turns.
- Focus on a strong pole plant.
- Focus on turning/pivoting your skis to skid/scrape off speed.
- Learn to edge 'check' your speed.
- Use your joints, ankles, knees and hips to stretch and bend, helping you maintain balance.
- Build confidence by skiing a few bumps at a time.

SKIING BUMPS

WHY?

- *Ski bumps slower, with total control.*
- *A movement constantly required in bumps to control and direct your speed and line.*
- *Ideal warm-up activity to get your feet turning.*

Pivoting Down the Bumps

HOW?

Think of a line down the slope. Aim to keep your feet on this line.

Turn your feet/legs/skis across this line. This produces a skid or scraping feeling of travelling sideways down the bump.

Push against the outer foot to check the sliding action. Pole plant.

Release the pressure and edge. Soften the legs in order to absorb the bump and turn your ski's back down the slope.

Keep steering and turning the legs, creating a series of controlled, short, skidding turns down the bumps.

The perfect tool to control your speed in bumps!

WHERE?

In bumps. Pisted slopes, reasonable gradient. Narrow, steeper, icy slopes. Practice on flat pistes then take into easy bumps.

TIPS

Focus

Focus on unwinding your legs whilst looking for the next bump to check against.

Imagery

Imagine a shallow snakelike line down the hill. Your aim is to keep your feet/skis pivoting on this line whilst flowing down the bumps like water.

Feedback

If you start gaining speed across the slope you have turned your feet too quickly at the start of the turn and have ended up edging too much. Focus on gradually unwinding and turning your feet/skis towards the next bump.

TOP TIP

Keep your feet independent and underneath you!

SKIING BUMPS

WHY?

Check, Pole, Slide.

- *Check your speed.*
- *Use the bumps to check against.*

HOW?

Push/Shove hard against the heel of the lower ski to check your speed. This will happen towards the back of the bump. Pole Plant.

Release the pressure/edge. Turn the skis a fraction down the slope. Do not rush.

Keep pivoting your ski's to create a skid/slide down the bump.....

...look for the next bump you want to check your speed against.

Push hard against the heel of the lower ski to check your speed, pole plant and unwind....

The 'check' happens at the end of one turn before the beginning of the next.

WHERE?

Practice on spaced out bumpier slopes. Use in bumps.

TIPS

Focus

Use your muscle strength, flex all three joints, ankles/knees/hips, to help you push against the lower ski and check your speed.

Imagery

A quick checking action is like a strong, fast, kicking movement. Imagine one leg turning and kicking out below you, this turns and pushes the ski on to an edge, acting like a brief breaking action.

Feedback

Having checked your speed, don't turn the skis/feet too much across the slope, otherwise you will end up on your edges gaining speed across the slope. Think of unwinding your legs gradually, enabling you to scrape/skid off speed.

TOP TIP
Check, pole, unwind and LOOK!

SKIING BUMPS

John Wayne Turns

WHY?

- *Learn to check quickly and keep turning the feet underneath you.*
- *Keep the feet wide, you can learn to turn the skis quicker.*

HOW?

Keep the feet/legs/skis hip width apart, check your speed, pole plant.

Push down on the pole as you soften/bend the leg you have just checked with, bend and turn this leg underneath you.

Keep the feet wide, start to push and turn the outer ski/foot to check your speed, pole plant.

Use the pole to help release the pressure and turn the inner leg underneath you.

Start to push and turn the lower ski/foot to check your speed...... and so on.

Keep the skis wide and boogie down the bumps 'John Wayne' style!

WHERE?

Start on smaller bumps and build your confidence towards bigger bumps.

TIPS

Focus

Focus on using the heel of your foot/back of the ski to shove and check your speed.

Imagery

Imagine being on a horse, 'John Wayne' style! The legs turning underneath you but working independently.

Feedback

As you check, if the edge of your ski gets stuck in the snow use a firm pole plant to help you push down to release the pressure and pivot around.

TOP TIP

It may not feel pretty but it works!

SKIING BUMPS

Hit the Rhythm

WHY?

- *Ski edge to edge short turns.*
- *Control your speed by quick, short turns.*

HOW?

Point your skis down the slope. Gain momentum, push against one ski creating an edge and slight checking action. Pole plant.

Having quickly jabbed the snow, release this pressure bringing the ski's back underneath you, look where the skis are facing.....down the hill!

Once again, jab the snow with your foot/ski, pushing quickly against the edge of this ski resulting in a brief braking action.

Release once more letting your legs bend back underneath you, ready to repeat the quick checking action again....

Get in to the rhythm of the bumps !

WHERE?

Practice on a pisted slope, slight gradient.

TIPS

Focus

Focus on using your heel or the back of the ski to jab the snow. The movement is a quick, strong action that pushes the edge of the ski in to the snow.

Imagery

Think of your skis being on a trampoline, as you push down against the trampoline your skis want to rise and lighten, let them, do not pivot them too much, just retract them. Then be ready to push down against the surface once more.

Feedback

Picking up too much speed? Turn the skis across the slope more to check your speed. Be aware that a strong check will result in a rebound action, use the rebound to bring the skis back underneath you before you actively check your speed again.

TOP TIP

Hit a rhythm... jab, pole, release, jab, pole, release.....

SKIING BUMPS

Boogie Down the Bumps

WHY?

- *A faster, more direct way to ski bumps.*
- *Edge to edge turns to control your speed.*
- *Absorb bumps and react to the terrain.*

HOW?

Focus on where you are going to make your first check.

Having quickly jabbed the snow, release this pressure bringing the foot/ski you have pushed against underneath you, look where the skis are facing..... down the hill.

Once again, jab the snow with your other foot/ski, pushing very quickly against the edge of this ski resulting in a brief braking action.

Release once more letting your legs bend back underneath, don't overturn them, be ready to repeat the quick checking action again....and so on.

Ski a more direct, faster line through the bumps.

WHERE?

Start on smaller bumps and build your confidence towards bigger bumps.

TIPS

Focus

Try to disregard the bumps and focus on the movements and rhythm for short turns.

Imagery

Imagine a narrow gully down the hill, aim to control your speed by rhythmically checking against the side walls of the gully using the heels of your feet/skis.

Feedback

If you are picking up too much speed, complete 3-4 short check turns, then bring yourself to a complete stop with a powerful check.

TOP TIP

The pole plant is a MUST, arms forwards and wrist strong.

QUICK TIPS!

PIVOT ROUND YOUR POLE

A major 'must' for the bumps! Having checked your speed you should be at the slowest point in your turn, push down on your pole and use this to help you pivot your feet/skis down the hill.

RED INK

Imagine red ink flowing through the bumps. This will help you see where the troughs of the bumps are. This is the quickest route through the bumps.
To slow your speed whilst travelling down this route, scrape off speed in between the bumps and use a 'check' towards the back of the oncoming bump.

ARM YOURSELF

Keep your arms in your peripheral vision. Exaggerate this, it really helps you commit to your pole plant, aiding your balance and enabling you to turn your feet/skis.

RIGHT BUMPS WRONG TUNE!

Remember how bumps are formed - by skiers skiing short turns. Different skiers will perform different short turns and hence set different rhythms to the bumps. You have to learn to adapt your own rhythm to someone else's - pick up that rhythm!

SKIING RUTS

To ski ruts select some shallower bumps to start with. Bring your feet closer together to help you flow through the ruts, you can still 'scrape off' and check your speed but learn to do this with the feet closer together. Build your confidence on shallower bumps then take the same movement pattern/rhythms to steeper bumps.

SKIING STEEPS

Skiing steeper slopes takes confidence and learning not to jam on the brakes! This section provides you with the best techniques to help control your speed when confronted with steep slopes! Practise and you will acquire the tools, ready to use when necessary. Your confidence will grow along with your skill, and enjoyment of the STEEPS!

TIPS FOR THE STEEPS!

- Learn to Scrape and Check.
- Don't jam on the brakes (edges).
- Keep the legs straight if you fall.

Pivoting – Use Your Brakes!

WHY?

- *Essential technique for steeps.*
- *The main action for deceleration.*
- *Learn to turn your feet/legs independently to your body.*

HOW?

Face your skis down the fall line. Pick up a little speed. Keep low, squat slightly, this will help you turn your legs and feet more independently to your body.

Actively turn your feet, legs and skis across the direction you are travelling. REMEMBER. Your skis are parallel but turn independently of one another.

This action will create a slide/skidding motion but still follow the route of the fall line.

As the slide/skid subsides turn your skis back towards the fall line. Repeat if you have the time and space. Practise this on steep slopes, so you gain confidence at sliding.

This is your 'get out of jail' card!

WHERE?

Cambered slopes/pathways.
Steeper, icy slopes, bumps.
Any tricky situation/location!

TIPS

Focus

No need to focus on edging! Your skis will edge automatically when you turn them.

Imagery

Imagine each foot has a nail right through the centre of your foot/instep. Your aim is to pivot your feet/skis around the nail.

Feedback

Keep your skis/feet working very independently, don't push the backs of the skis together in order to turn the skis across the slope.

TOP TIP

Think powerful, active rotation! It's the tool for the steeps!

Scrape then Check

WHY?

- ***Reduces your speed completely.***
- ***Use this platform to change direction and hop.***

HOW?

On a steeper slope pivot the feet/legs/skis powerfully to produce a scraping action that will help slow you.

Whilst scraping, start to push against the inside edge of your lower ski/foot. Think of pushing your lower ski slightly further away from you but maintain your balance over it.

As you push against this edge, allow your ankles, knees and hips to bend in order to keep in balance, plant the pole.

Push down positively on the pole to help your movement upwards, releasing the edges and allowing you to lighten your skis to change direction.

Scrape off the speed and enjoy the slide!

WHERE?

Steeper slopes, on piste/off piste

TIPS

Focus

Focus on keeping your feet/legs/skis independent.

Imagery

On firmer terrain the skis will scrape easily, on softer snow you will stop more abruptly. On rubble/crud, the ride will feel as if you are on a slope full of stones and will take longer to establish a platform. Don't panic, keep pushing and feeling for the outer skis edge.

Feedback

As your feet scrape across the snow they may shudder. Control the shudder by your muscle strength, if you push too hard, too early and too aggressively you will edge and accelerate rather than decelerate.

TOP TIP

A firm pole plant is a must!

Pole Pressure !

WHY?

- *To Check your speed.*
- *Support your motion.*
- *Stabilize your movements.*
- *Hop to change direction.*

HOW?

Having scraped off your speed, push against the outer ski to form a platform, bring your pole forward ready to use.

The pole is planted when you check and have reduced your speed to practically zero. Use your ankles, knees and hips to help you check, keeping the arm and wrist firm on the pole.

Push upwards through your legs and downwards on your pole. The skis lighten as you push firmly down on the pole. Let the legs unwind to change direction.

Release the pole, making sure you are not dragging or leaning on it, whilst steering the skis towards the next turn.

Having reduced your speed and momentum, your feet may be at a standstill but your pole needs to be at the ready !

WHERE?

Pisted, steep slopes.
Off piste, steep slopes, bumps.

TIPS

Focus

Focus on controlling your speed first. Then move your attention to your pole.

Imagery

Imagine a pole vaulters pole action. The pole is planted at a point and at an angle, this stops the vaulters momentum, sending them upwards whilst the pole moves upright. The vaulter pushes downwards until the pole can no longer help support them....sounds familiar !

Feedback

Don't try to reach or find a particular point to plant your pole. With your arms forward, keeping your torso strong, you will plant the pole where it will help the most.

TOP TIP

Use the pole to push down on, take height and pivot around.

Jumping/How to Hop

WHY?

- ***The quickest way on steeps to change direction.***
- ***Change direction from a standstill.***

HOW?

Flex all three joints, ankles, knees and hips, to help feel for the outer ski to check your speed and anticipate your pole plant. This creates a strong platform to jump from.

As you uncoil and extend your legs, push downwards on your pole, resulting in the skis becoming lighter. Lift the heels of the skis slightly if in soft snow or on a very steep slope.

Turn your feet and skis whilst they are light and weightless.

Land softly, flexing the legs to help. Start to feel for your outer ski immediately, turning the feet, legs and skis to direct your line and control your speed, before checking again.

Some easy rules on how to jump and change direction on steeps.

WHERE?

Steeper, pisted slopes.
Steep slopes, on piste/off piste and bumps.

TIPS

Focus

Focus on jumping upwards and turning the feet/skis underneath you, rather than trying to turn the skis completely across the slope. The skis only need to turn towards the fall line.

Imagery

Think of a spring being compressed as you are checking your speed and uncoiling as you jump upwards.

Feedback

Finding it difficult to hop/unweight? Your speed must be at its slowest when you go to hop, it is very difficult to hop off a moving ski with no platform.

TOP TIP

Don't use the hop to control your speed (unless in a narrow couloir!)

One Footed Take Off!

WHY?

- ***When it gets even steeper......***
- ***Use the top ski more to support, balance and hop off!***

HOW?

Flex and sink as you check your speed, pole at the ready....

As you start to push down on your pole, stand, extend and push downwards against your top ski, bending and retracting the leg of the downhill ski.

Turn the skis slightly down the hill.

Land softly on both skis ready to steer and control your speed and line........

Helps change direction on the steeps, plus....it looks good!

WHERE?

Steeper slopes, on/off piste.

TIPS

Focus

Focus on pushing down against the top ski and actively turning the lower ski.

Imagery

Think of going up stairs. You push down on one foot (top ski), extending this leg whilst bending and lifting the other leg to reach for the next step.

Feedback

This technique is more useful on steeper slopes, or when you have reduced your speed so much that you have lost your rhythm and momentum.

TOP TIP

Turn the lower ski/foot to help your skis change direction.

QUICK TIPS!

SIDE SLIP TO SAFETY

If your anxieties take over, the thought of turning makes you feel sick or you just lose your nerve. DON'T PANIC. Use one of the most important tools in the box. SIDE SLIP your way to safety. Face the skis across the slope and maintain a firm, wide stance. Release the edges to allow you to lose some height. If the snow is heavy then you may have to really force the snow beneath you to help you slide. Make sure you use your top ski for support, do not place all your weight on your lower ski.

SPEED CONTROL

Use a steep enough slope that does not psyche you out. Work on your speed control. Aim your skis directly down the slope, rotate your legs/feet/skis independently and powerfully underneath you. This creates a skidding/sliding motion. Start to push on the outer ski creating more edge and a platform that will completely stop your speed!

NARROW & STEEP

When you run out of space you may need to jump the skis from edge to edge. Use your strength to jump upwards and turn your skis directly across the slope. Land softly with the feet a good distance apart, both skis must help support your mass. Do not try and balance over the lower ski.

TOP SKI SUPPORT

On steep slopes you must use both skis/legs to balance with. Having changed direction, make sure you land and steer with your skis/legs independently. If you topple off balance use the top ski to balance against even if you lean against it and have to sit down on the slope, it is safer to do this than fall directly down the slope.

SKIING OFF PISTE

'Off Piste' skiing now matches on piste skiing in popularity. Spurred on by the snowboarding market, modern ski technique and equipment has been revolutionised. Skis have been designed specifically to ski variable and off piste conditions, whilst not being solely for use off piste, helping skiers gain confidence and experience in the 'all mountain' environment.

Skiing off piste requires you to adapt your technique to the variable conditions. Snow conditions change constantly, temperatures, gradient, weather, wind, depth of snow, visability etc, all have an impact on how you ski. When skiing off piste you must be aware of these ever changing conditions, adapting your own technique accordingly whilst remaining totally aware of yours and other skiers safety.

This section provides several ways of tackling differing snow conditions and slopes. These tips are here to help you deal with conditions you may encounter when skiing the mountain and more specifically off piste. However, whether learning to power through heavier snow or float on top of deeper powder it is paramount to be aware of safety on the slopes.

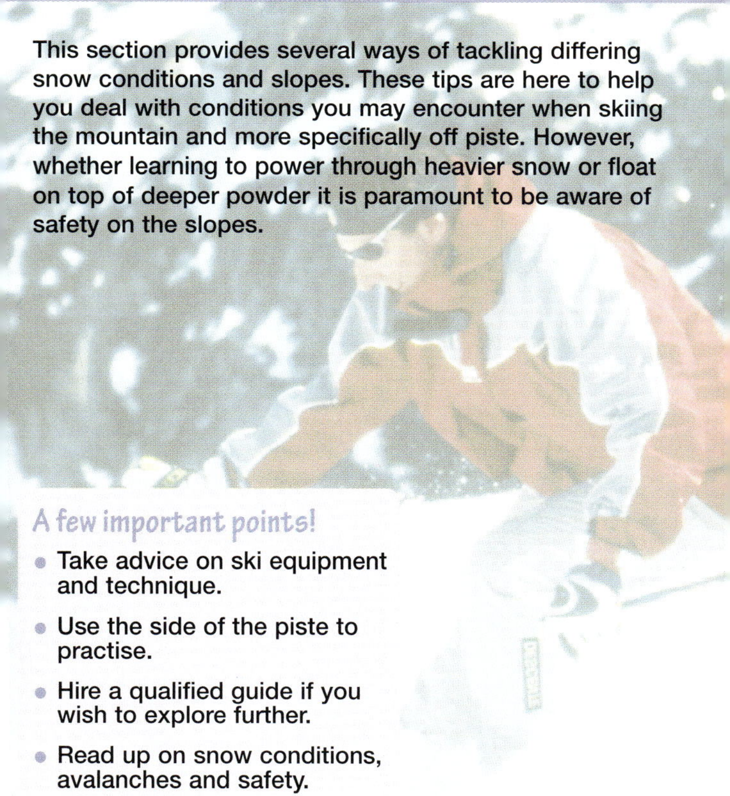

A few important points!

- Take advice on ski equipment and technique.
- Use the side of the piste to practise.
- Hire a qualified guide if you wish to explore further.
- Read up on snow conditions, avalanches and safety.
- Invest in the right gear.
- If in doubt, don't ski it.

Mountain Safety

Mountain Awareness & Safety

We have put together some basic information if you are aiming to ski off piste. It is advisable to seek expert advice and help if you are intending to ski further afield than slopes near to the pisted areas. Either way we hope it will encourage you to be properly prepared when you begin to venture further afield, off piste, perhaps as far as the territory sometimes referred to as 'the backcountry'.

Nature, especially in the mountains, deserves our respect. Too many people venture out unaware of the dangers that abound in the backcountry. This lack of knowledge can be deadly, here is some basic, but essential, information for staying safe when travelling in the backcountry.

Backcountry Safety Code

- It is strongly recommended that you ski in the backcountry with a mountain guide. IFMGA qualified.
- Never travel off-piste without adequate insurance. Most standard winter sports insurance policies do not cover for going off-piste. Find an insurance company that can provide the correct cover and check the small print.
- Never ski alone – always ski in a group and always ensure that your goals are realistic and achievable by the whole group. Do not endanger yourself, your group or others on the mountain.
- Before setting out ensure you have collected information about the weather, snow conditions and recent avalanche activity. Listen to the experts and ask for advice. If in doubt, don't ski it.
- Equip yourself properly. Always check that your bindings release properly and your other gear is in good order. Always ski with the essential safety gear - avalanche transceiver, shovel and probe.
- Stay humble. Keep a sharp eye and ear out and heed your own instincts. Always ski within the limits of your ability.

- Pick your route carefully & be prepared to handle changing situations – with other skiers and with the mountain and the conditions.
- Human factors are the most common cause of accidents on the mountain - fatigue, complacency, over-confidence, single-minded lust for powder. Listen to your instinct and don't take unnecessary risks.
- Always obey signs – they provide vital information for you and your safety on the mountain.

Equipment

Recent years have seen big changes in ski equipment design and technology. Whereas in the past, ski touring equipment was really only recommended for hardened ski-mountaineers, this is no longer the case. Spurred on by the snowboard revolution, the major manufacturers have developed a wide selection of alpine off piste and touring skis, boots and bindings (also known as "Randonnee" equipment) which make off-piste skiing and ski touring much more accessible.

Safety equipment: When venturing off-piste you must always carry the essential items of safety equipment: transceiver, shovel and probe.

The transceiver is a radio device that is used to pinpoint the whereabouts of other skiers after an avalanche. Always wear your transceiver, ensure it is switched on and be sure to know how to use it.

A sectional probe assembles to form a 2-3 meter probe and is useful to quickly determine the exact location of a buried skier.

The shovel – a lightweight aluminium, collapsible model is best – is then used to quickly dig out the victim.

A simple and lightweight pack with a capacity of no more than 35 litres is also essential. A model with ski attachments is recommended.

Learn to respect the mountain environment, seek advice, enjoy your skiing experiences and above all be safe!

Compiled by expert mountain guide, Nick Parks
www.mountaintracks.co.uk

Stem Step

WHY?

- ***Change edges/direction easily using a stem step.***
- ***Feel the snow's texture and commit to the turn.***

HOW?

Use the shape of the curve to direct your line and control your speed.

When you want to change direction step the upper ski out, bringing your pole forwards to plant.

Place the ski on to the snow on its new edge, do not edge too much, allow your inner leg to continue to support you.

Lighten the inner leg as you pole plant and change direction. Pressurise and steer the outer foot

Turn the inner leg back to parallel aiding your balance. Concentrate on maintaining the curve and staying strong over the outer ski.

Gain confidence when changing direction in variable, difficult snow conditions. Test the territory!

WHERE?

Soft off piste slopes, not too deep.
Bumpy, variable snow conditions.
Slushy snow.

TIPS

Focus

Focus on steering the curve. Use the outer foot/ski to push through the soft/slushy snow.

Imagery

Imagine you are skiing on a fine layer of icing.
When you go to step your ski, feel through the layers of the snow, give yourself time as you start to change direction and find the most stable, firm layer to support yourself on.

Feedback

No need to step the ski too wide, feel for the edge of the ski as you place the ski on the snow, be ready to push gradually but not too aggressively.

TOP TIP

Do not bang your foot down, place and feel through the snow!

Light On Your Feet

WHY?

- ***Learn to feel through the snow.***
- ***Keep light on your feet.***

HOW?

Select a slope not too steep or bumpy but with soft snow. Aim your skis down the slope to pick up a little momentum.

Steer the skis in a small curve/arc, applying pressure through your feet.

Having pressured the skis downward against the snow, the snow pushes the skis back up, allow this to happen so the skis become light.

Land softly, using your joints to aid balance but be ready to push down once more, through your feet/skis, against the snow.

As soon as you feel pressure back, help your skis lighten by extending your legs.

Lighten the load in shallow, variable snow.

WHERE?

Shallow off piste.
Light, not deep, cruddy or heavy snow.

TIPS

Focus

Bring the feet/skis a little closer together but work them independently. Feel pressure through both feet, towards the instep/heels of your feet.

Imagery

Your aim is to glide over the snow not deep within it. React and use the snow to help you feel light and weightless, not heavy and lethargic!

Feedback

Do not pivot the feet/skis in the snow to change direction or steer your curve. Change direction when the skis are light and weightless. Use the outer ski to direct your curve. Use the inner ski actively for support and stability.

TOP TIP

Use your suspension (ankles, knees and hips) to keep balancing!

Freeride With Power

WHY?

- *Use speed to power through heavier, firmer off piste.*
- *Enjoy longer, faster turns off piste.*

HOW?

Set off down the hill, then gradually curve back up the hill. Feel the condition of the snow as you do this. Does it feel easy to carve through or difficult? Do you have a firm base to push against, or not? Your first turn gives you the opportunity to test the snow conditions.

Jump or pull your feet/skis out of the snow to change direction. Essential if the snow feels heavy, cruddy, slushy, or if you have no speed.

Land softly, feel the conditions of the snow under your feet/skis. Use your arms to help your balance. Maintain a strong stance, keeping your body alligned with your skis.

Dominate your equipment. Feel the pressure, through the instep and heel of your feet, against both your skis.

Drive the skis through the snow maintaining a curve to gradually reduce your speed.

Use the curve to power through heavier, off piste.

WHERE?

Open terrain that is safe, no rocks, trees or other objects. Not ideal for deep powder or steeps.

TIPS

Focus

Be dominant and strong over your skis. Do not pivot the feet/skis in this snow, this could very easily cause injury to the knee. Use the shape of the curve to control your speed.

Imagery

Imagine a knife slicing through thick icing on a cake. Once the knife has cut through there maybe a firm fruit cake below this or possibly a soft sponge. If it's a sponge your knife will suddenly become light and you will have to control the slicing action. If the next layer is a fruit cake then you may have to push harder in order to cut through the cake. Snow textures and layers change like this and you have to react with your skis accordingly.

Feedback

If you find yourself on your edges with no pressure against your skis, fight to bring your balance back over your feet. Use your stomach muscles and core strength to regain balance.

TOP TIP

Dominate and drive the skis through the snow.

Powder Play

WHY?

- *The technique to use in deep, steep, light powder snow.*
- *Use the reaction from the snow to help you change direction.*

HOW?

Place the skis/feet closer together, push down evenly on both feet. You will get a reaction pushing the skis back up to the surface. At this point turn your feet to change your direction.

As you sink back down into the snow, steer the skis in a curve underneath you, pushing against both skis more evenly.

Once again, utilise the reaction back from the snow to bend the legs, release pressure and turn the skis back towards the fall line.

Sink once more, use your pole plant to help establish a rhythm.

When the skis are at their lightest, turn the feet/skis before you sink again.

Play in powder, do not be afraid of falling. It's trial, error and fun!

WHERE?

Side of the piste.
Fresh fallen snow on pisted slopes.
Deep, light, powdery snow.

TIPS

Focus

You will constantly be thrown back and forth against your boots whilst skiing off piste, balancing is on going. Remember, it is the shape of the curve that controls your speed and the depth of the snow itself.

Imagery

Think of a trampet that has a bar you can support yourself on. As your feet/legs bounce up from the trampet you feel weightless, in mid air. You reach your highest point, gravity takes over, your body falls and your feet and legs absorb your landing ready to push against the trampet again – skiing powder resembles this feeling.

Feedback

Picking up too much speed? Ski wider curves, work on your steering and as you gain confidence start to make the curves more acute.

TOP TIP

Only change direction when you feel in control of your speed.

Deeper, Heavier, Steeper

WHY?

- ***When the slope is steeper and the snow heavier or deeper use strength to control your descent.***

HOW?

Your first turn in steeper, deeper, heavier snow is the most difficult. Kick your skis out of the snow to face the skis more down the slope.

Use your leg and body strength to pull the skis out of the snow and change direction. You may try to turn the skis more across the snow, due to the steepness and weight of the snow.

As you sink back into the snow, feel for the outer ski to push against and check your speed. Use the inside leg for support. The mass of the snow will help slow you down as well.

Push against your pole and use your momentum to help you retract your skis and legs out of the soft snow once more.

Each turn may feel different due to the variable conditions of the snow but try to feel for a rhythm.

Be more forceful, use your strength when the going gets STEEP!

WHERE?

In the thick of it!
Trial and error here!

TIPS

Focus

Don't try and rush your turns, still focus on controlling your speed before you aim to jump the skis out of the snow and change direction.

Imagery

Concentrate on your breathing. Your muscles are working harder, so keep calm and breath evenly. Pick a melody or slow song to hum as you descend.

Feedback

As you land in the softer, heavier snow, pull your lower arm around in front of you. This helps maintain your balance and provides a stronger aligned position over your supporting foot and ski.

TOP TIP
Keep the skis and legs working independently.

QUICK TIPS!

POLE CHECK

Before you ski an off piste slope use your pole to give you information about the snow beneath you. Stab the pole through the snow and feel for the layers beneath (use the handle end of the pole if easier). See how far you have to go before you hit a firm base. Learn to read and feel the different layers and qualities of snow, it will give you feedback on how best to ski it.

OBJECTS!

Be aware and watchful for any lumps and bumps whilst skiing off piste. These could be anything from rocks to tree stumps. Learn to watch in front of you and make quick decisions as you ski.

SIDE OF THE PISTE

You can often find some great off piste snow to the side of most pistes. Check for any objects and whether the gradient of the slope is suitable for you. Even if it has been skied already it is a great way to become more practised with the knowledge that if you tire or feel you are out of control you have an emergency exit to hand. Such off piste skiing provides opportunity to 'snack on' this type of skiing without committing yourself.

FALLING

If you feel yourself falling, try and keep the legs straight, this will prevent them being twisted unnecessarily.

FINDING A SKI

If you lose a ski, see if you can look back at your tracks and re-trace these. Walking in off piste is very tiring, take your time, use your poles to help stab downwards and feel anything firm that could be your lost ski. Buy and use powder leashes when skiing off piste, they will help enormously.

STEEPNESS OF SLOPE

When on steep, off piste slopes ski the slope as a steep slope. Use scraping and checking techniques to slow you down and jumping to help you change direction.

CRUD

When snow has a dense crust to it or feels so heavy that you cannot steer your skis at all, use either a kick turn or a jump turn to change your direction and a traverse to cross the slope and gradually lose height.

INSTRUCTIONAL
DVD'S from the
WARREN SMITH SKI ACADEMY
www.warrensmith-skiacademy.com
LIFE AFTER SKI SCHOOL...
NEW RELEASE - LESSON 3
WARREN SMITH SKI ACADEMY
more !
carving
steeps
moguls
freeride
TECHNIQUE SOLUTIONS FOR INTERMEDIATE, ADVANCED AND INSTRUCTOR LEVEL SKIERS
LESSON 3
DVD
WARREN SMITH SKI ACADEMY
carving
steeps
moguls
freeride
TECHNIQUE SOLUTIONS FOR INTERMEDIATE AND ADVANCED SKIERS
LESSON 1
DVD
WARREN SMITH SKI ACADEMY
more...
carving
steeps
moguls
freeride
TECHNIQUE SOLUTIONS FOR INTERMEDIATE AND ADVANCED SKIERS
LESSON 2
DVD
Ski technique solutions for intermediate, advanc and expert skiers. DVD look at Carving, Steeps Moguls and Freeride. Recommeded in Daily M Sunday Times, Esquire, Men's Health, Stuff, Ski Club of Great Britain, Ifyouski.com, Financial Times and Virgin Radio.
Mail Order today:
UK office +44 (0)1525 374757
sales@snowsportsynergy.com
demo clips at www.ifyouski.com/technique
VISA
EUROCARD MasterCard
VIDE

Acknowledgements

My special thanks to Paul & Tom Major for their help, patience, love and good humour.

Published by Pock'it Books
Tel: 01279 778905
Email: info@pockitbooks.co.uk
www.pockitbooks.co.uk

Inspired To Ski Courses www.inspiredtoski.com
Email: info@inspiredtoski.com

Designed and printed by Red Ink, Ipswich 01473 230600

"A brilliant and simple idea.."
Mail on Sunday Dec 2002

"..techniques continue to evolve and move away from the old school styles, there is now a fantastic addition to any skier's "toolkit" in the form of a new book written by top British teacher Sally Chapman.."
Scottish Courier, Nov 2003

Sally Chapman

is one of Britains leading ski teachers, a trainer for the British Association of Snowsports Instructors and director of Inspired To Ski. Those who have been taught by Sally will confirm that her enthusiasm and joy of teaching skiing is inspirational. Sally's honest energy and enthusiasm is captured in the'Pock'It Instructor' series, combined with her expertise and huge experience, the booklets provide an excellent aid for skiers to broaden their horizons and ski the whole mountain.

Hit the slopes with your 'Pock'It Instructor' this winter!